Old KIRRIEMUIR

by
Fiona Mackenzie

Queen's Park Football Club was just one of the many football clubs in Kirriemuir. Its members are shown here with two trophies following their victory in the Kirriemuir Juvenile Cup in 1929. Some of Kirriemuir's other football teams have included Kirrie Thistle, Kirrie Hearts, Maryton Rovers, Kirrie Violets and Thrums.

With the exception of the pictures on pages 18, 21, 33, 36, 38 and 40, which are reproduced by courtesy of Alan Brotchie, all the images in this book have been reproduced from the collection of Angus Council Cultural Services. If you would like copies of any of these pictures, please contact: Angus Local Studies Centre, Montrose Library, 214 High Street, Montrose, DD10 9RS. www.angus.gov.uk/history

ACKNOWLEDGEMENT
The author would like to acknowledge the help of Mr David Fawcett in the preparation of this book.

The building standing at the junction of Bank Street and the town square remained at this spot until 1910. A potentially lethal incident took place there in the middle of the nineteenth century when it was being used as an ironmonger's. The building caught fire and local people were helping to remove its contents when they realised that gunpowder was stored there. Changing tactics, many of the helpers ran towards Northmuir to escape the possibility of the gunpowder exploding! However, disaster was averted and from then on storing gunpowder in the centre of town was banned. During World War II an air raid shelter was situated in the same position.

INTRODUCTION

Kirriemuir's roots stretch far back in history, and the town is well-known across the world for the numerous famous people who have been born there. However, very little is known about Kirriemuir in prehistoric times, although a few remnants of its early history still exist. One well-known feature is a standing stone on the Hill, known simply as the Stannin' Stane and possibly dating back to the Bronze Age. Tillyloss, situated just off Brechin Road, gives another tantalising clue about early settlement as the name is probably derived from the Gaelic *tulach-lios*. This means a rounded knoll with an inhabited enclosure, and suggests that Iron Age roundhouses may have once stood on this site.

The Roman army certainly had a presence in the area around the modern town, as pieces of Roman road found in Caddam Wood and other nearby sites confirm. However, it was not until 1201 that the name of Kirriemuir was recorded in writing. At that time Earl Gillechrist, the first Earl of Angus, gave the 'chapels, lands, tithes, common pasturage aisements, and all the pertinents belonging to the Church of Kerimor' to Arbroath Abbey. Since 1201 there have been over 30 different spellings of the name, including Keirmure, Killemure and Kerymor.

The fact that an Earl of Angus had such a close relationship with Kirriemuir in 1201 suggests that he was the patron of the church at Kirriemuir. This connection probably extended back into Pictish times when the equivalent title to that of earl was 'mormaer'. If so, the Church of 'Kerimor', and indeed the immediate area, would probably have been an important Pictish site. This speculation certainly corresponds with the large number of Pictish stones – so far totalling eighteen – that have been discovered in and around the Old Parish Church.

Kirriemuir grew up around the church, and the area known as the Roods was probably the first part where conscious town planning occurred. This would have been in the twelfth or thirteenth century. In 1459 the town was made a burgh of barony, a development associated with the growing power of the House of Douglas (i.e. the Earls of Angus), which controlled the barony of Kirriemuir at that time. The rights and privileges of a burgh of barony varied and were different to those of a burgh town, and Kirriemuir had no right of foreign trade but was allowed weekly markets, resident craftsmen, the power to buy and sell, and a market cross. Kirriemuir is the only burgh of barony in Angus.

Following a royal mandate in 1352, officials from Dundee were allowed to protect their trading interests by going to Kirriemuir to publicly forbid trading in the town and seize the goods of offenders. This indicates that the town's manufacturing output was already significant by this stage; indeed, its textile industry became a crucial source of employment for centuries. Handloom weaving in cottages gave way to textile factories in the nineteenth century when Stewart & Ogilvy's Gairie Linen Works and Wilkie's Kirriemuir Linen Works became the town's main employers.

Kirriemuir's proximity to the Glens and their drove roads also ensured that agriculture and the movement of cattle played an important part in the town's development. Markets, allowed by the town's burgh of barony status, swelled its population. The influence of farming continues to the present day, although the potato and berry fields that were once found in the Northmuir area were replaced by housing during the last few decades of the twentieth century.

Kirriemuir's title of 'Gateway to the Glens' is apposite. The beautiful glens of Isla, Prosen and Clova can be reached easily from the town, and links between the town and rural communities in the Glens are still strong.

Throughout its history Kirriemuir has produced several characters of note, and has also had strong musical connections. Perhaps the best-known Kirriemarian is Sir J. M. Barrie, author of the play *Peter Pan*, while Bon Scott, equally famous in the world of rock music, was also born in Kirriemuir. He was the lead singer of rock group AC/DC from 1974 until his death in 1980.

Songs listened to and performed all over the world have their roots in Kirriemuir and draw people to the town. The *Ball of Kirriemuir* is infamous and its story is known far and wide, although the original ballad has been changed so much since it was first sung that its Scots language has become very diluted. The Scottish dance tune Caddam Wood also brings fame to the town. Every year the Kirriemuir Folk Festival attracts a wide audience and continues to keep a strong connection to traditional music alive in the town.

Perhaps Kirriemuir's most curious link is with Hawaii. Three local brothers emigrated there in the late 1870s and started something of a trend. Many of those who followed their lead found employment on sugar plantations. The number of emigrants became so significant that twenty-five percent of Hawaiians of Scottish descent have forbears from the area in and around Kirriemuir.

From prehistoric times to the present day Kirriemuir has produced a great deal of fascinating architectural, social and economic history. The heritage that has survived must be preserved, so that local people and visitors of the future can continue to appreciate the town's unique qualities.

Kirrie Den is a well-known park that was gifted to the town in the second half of the nineteenth century by George Wilkie and Sir Leonard Lyell. It lies on the banks of the Gairie Burn, and is unusual in being secluded in a hollow yet close to the hustle and bustle of the town centre. Known simply as the Den, it is surrounded by sites of interest including Court Hillock and the Witch Pool. The former was the site of the regality court before its removal to the Town House in the seventeenth century. This court was presided over by baron bailies on behalf of the town's landlord – which for generations was the House of Douglas – and was called a regality court because it could deal with cases that elsewhere could only be considered by a royal court. One of the earliest references to the regality court in Kirriemuir dates from 1488. The Witch Pool was a pool of water on the Court Hillock where witches were supposedly drowned. Above the Den stood the Meikle Mill. This was originally driven by the waters of the Gairie, but by 1865 steam power had been introduced to turn the milling machinery. The mill, which produced oat flakes, was sold to J. A. Whamond & Sons in 1919, along with the Angus Mill in the Glengate. After various takeovers and name-changes production ceased in 1991 and the Meikle Mill was demolished to make way for housing.

Generations of families have enjoyed using Kirrie Den as a place for picnics, a playground, or simply as somewhere to enjoy the sun on a summer's day. This includes not only local families but also visitors to the town for whom the Den is a great attraction. Kirriemuir was, and still is, a popular holiday destination for people from all over Scotland and England. Indeed, before foreign holidays became commonplace in the 1960s, many visitors came from towns and cities not very far away, including Dundee, and many Dundonians still have fond memories of their holidays in Kirriemuir. Postcards from the early 1900s onwards show that the Den was considered to be one of the prime attractions in the town.

2669.

THE TANNAGE BRAE, KIRRIEMUIR.

A tannery and boot factory gave its name to Tannage Brae, although like many streets in Kirriemuir this one has had more than one name, being called Bridge Street prior to 1910. The *Statistical Account of Scotland* of 1792 states that at that time around 1,200 pairs of shoes were being made annually for export in the Tannage Brae factory. The factory, which closed in 1908, represented one aspect of Kirriemuir's industrial past, the other major component being the textile industry. The buildings in the dip on the right of this view occupy the site of the former tannery.

Glamis Road leads from Kirriemuir to the village of Glamis and ultimately to Dundee. The present St Andrew's Church on Glamis Road was built in 1903. Southmuir Primary School was also formerly situated on this street, having been built in 1836 as Webster's Seminary. John Webster was a banker and writer in Kirriemuir who bequeathed money to erect and maintain a school. When the modern Webster's High School was built in 1954 the old building became the primary department of that school, and then became Southmuir Primary in 1973. In 2001 Southmuir Primary School moved into a new building alongside Webster's High School, and the former building was abandoned. Many of Kirriemuir's churches operated schools during the nineteenth century; for instance the South Free Church ran the South Free School. St Mary's School, attached to the church of the same name, was built in 1854 and enlarged twice before its closure in the 1920s.

The name Bellie's Brae is a corruption of Baillie's or Bailie's Brae. During the eighteenth century the baron bailies held courts of regality at the Town House, which still sits at the top of Bellie's Brae today. In this picture the gasworks office can be seen in the left foreground, while the prominent steeple belongs to the Old Parish Church. The steeple was built in 1790 and was the gift of Charles Lyell, Laird of Kinnordy and grandfather of Charles Lyell the geologist.

The original bell was replaced by the present one in 1839. The Old Parish Church has a long and distinguished history, having been granted to Arbroath Abbey as the church of 'Kerimor' by Earl Gillechrist in 1201. When the present church was completed in 1788 its Pictish origins were further confirmed by the discovery of ninth or tenth century Pictish stones in the foundations of the previous building. It was known as the Barony Kirk from 1929 until 1972, at which point it united with St Ninian's, and is now called The Glens and Old Parish Church.

The word brae means a steep bank or hillside, and Bellie's Brae is one of several streets that highlight how hilly Kirriemuir's landscape is. Important industrial premises were formerly situated on either side of Bellie's Brae. The gasworks was located here from the 1840s until its closure in the 1950s – during the 1960s the gas holders were removed and a car park was later built on the site. However, the Kirriemuir Gas (Light) Company's office building survived the closure of the works and is now the home of the town's aviation museum. This is an independent museum which was established in 1985 by Richard Moss, a former member of the Royal Air Force. Still dominating Bellie's Brae and facing the site of the gasworks is J. & D. Wilkie's textile factory. This was originally known as the Gairie Linen Works and was opened in 1872 by Stewart & Ogilvy. Wilkie's Kirriemuir Linen Works were originally situated on Marywell Brae and opened in the late 1860s. The two companies merged in 1972.

The Town House stands in the middle of the town square and dates back to 1604, although considerable architectural alterations to its original rectangular shape in the nineteenth century gave rise to the rounded walls seen now. On the right-hand side of this picture Kirriemuir Soda Fountain and the former Regal Cinema can be seen. These two businesses were run by the well-known Visocchi family. The Regal operated from 1911 until the late 1960s, and between 1913 and 1919 there was also a cinema in Morrison Street. Some of the buildings in the area illustrated here were later knocked down to widen the road. A business in the town which is well-known for its confectionery delights is the Star Rock Shop, which is situated in the Roods. David Ferguson opened the shop in 1833, naming it after the 'Starry Rock' that he sold. This got its name because of the star-like shapes which appeared on sections of the rock as a result of the way it was rolled.

Many businesses came and went from the High Street but a few stood the test of time, albeit moving from site to site. James Norrie printed the *Kirriemuir Free Press and Advertiser* from 1884 onwards at 39 High Street. The *Kirriemuir Observer* was started in 1869, and was printed by W. B. Mills, who was the other printer and stationer in the town. In 1939 the two newspapers merged under the *Free Press* name and Norrie's continued to print the paper until 1974. W. B. Mills was a very well-known character in the area. He inherited his family's interest in journalism, following his grandfather (also W. B. Mills) and father (J. F. Mills) into the family's book, stationery, and printing business. He was also a member of a billiards team known in Kirriemuir as 'the Clean Sweeps' because in the late 1930s they were undefeated in competitive play for many years. The Town House (now Kirriemuir Gateway to the Glens Museum) housed W. B. Mills' business at one time, and has been home to many other businesses during the twentieth century. Several chemists have occupied the building including Buchanan's, Martin's, and latterly Kidd's.

High Street, Kirriemuir. 72928. JV

Markets were a frequent occurrence in past centuries, and many of them took place in the town square. The right to hold a market in the town and erect a market cross was conferred in 1459 by King James II when he made Kirriemuir a burgh of barony. At the weekly market days during the nineteenth century all sorts of commodities were on sale including pigs, poultry, butter and eggs. The Mucklie market was held in December and June. This was a feeing market where people were hired for all types of work including as servants and agricultural workers. There were also many other stalls with goods on show including confectionery, toys and jewellery, while more exotic attractions included a machine for testing your strength and the chance to see men dressed up as Zulu warriors. Although the Zulus were said to be genuine, it was alleged that one seen on show in Kirriemuir during a Mucklie in the 1880s was in fact from Brechin!

Just a few steps away from the town square visitors to Kirriemuir can discover numerous wynds and closes. Hugging the edge of the Old Parish Church, and just behind the Town House, is Kirk Wynd. This is probably the oldest street in Kirriemuir. It boasts several unusual architectural features including a marriage lintel dated 1688 and a straight arch at the opening of Grant's Pend. Kirriemuir contains a few wynds (wynd is a Scottish term used to describe a narrow lane or alley), another of which is St Malcolm's Wynd. There are two St Malcolms in Scottish history, the first being Malcolm, King of Scots (ruling from AD 1057 to 1093) and the second being King Malcolm IV (ruling from AD 1153 to 1165). However, the town has no known connection with either of these men. It is interesting to note that the name Malcolm translates as 'servant of Colm', or follower of Columba, and that St Colme's Close is nearby. Just beyond Grant's Pend in Kirk Wynd is Cat's Close, so called because it is extremely narrow. Cumberland Close is situated on the opposite side of the High Street and was formerly called Lindsay's Close. Legend has it that it gained its new name because after the Battle of Culloden in 1746 the Duke of Cumberland spent the night in the Old Gairie Inn, which was probably situated in Cumberland Close.

Bank Street was formerly called St Mary's Street. The name-change, which occurred during the nineteenth century, reflected the fact that the British Linen Bank stood on the street at the time. Many local people strongly objected to the change, and the body of opinion hoping to have the name reverted to St Mary's Street was perhaps at its most vocal in the late nineteenth and early twentieth centuries when frequent letters to local newspapers demanded action. Along with banks there have been numerous public houses and hotels on Bank Street. The Thrums Hotel was originally called the Temperance Hotel and was owned by the Scottish Temperance League; not surprisingly it only served soft drinks. Other hotels on Bank Street have included the Union Hotel which later became Hook's Hotel, the Commercial Hotel, and the Railway Inn. School Wynd lies at the eastern end of Bank Street, and formed the eastern boundary of Kirriemuir prior to the early eighteenth century when it was a small hamlet known as Kirkton of Kirriemuir. The name School Wynd alludes to the fact that the earliest known school in Kirriemuir was situated there. This was ruinous by 1784.

Bank Street lies to the north of the Old Parish Church and has various religious connections. The Auld Licht Kirk in Bank Street was created after a difference of opinion in 1806 led to members of the Secession Church splitting into the 'Auld Lichts' and 'New Lichts'. The controversy concerned the Westminster Confession, and how strictly every word of the confession should be adhered to. The Auld Lichts (mentioned in the work of Sir J. M. Barrie) chose to stick to original Secession principles. Their kirk in Bank Street was demolished and rebuilt in 1893 and the new building later became the site of the Free Evangelical (Baptist) Church. Bank Street United Presbyterian Church was originally converted from the Trades Hall by the Relief congregation in 1832. The building was sold to the St Mary's Episcopal Church congregation after their church in the Roods burned down in 1902. When they later moved to a new church they sold the Bank Street building, which has subsequently been occupied by various businesses including Franchi's restaurant and billiard room. St Colme's Close runs onto Bank Street, and a map of Kirriemuir in 1865 labelled a nearby area as 'site of chapel'. The chapel was possibly dedicated to St Columba, and could relate to an attempt to introduce a Scots saint to a previously Pictish religious centre. The building that was used as the Hanky School is also on Bank Street. J. M. Barrie was a pupil there when he was six years old. The name of the school was derived from the fact that pupils were required to bring a handkerchief to kneel on when saying prayers.

HIGH STREET, KIRRIEMUIR.

2722

This area of the town links the High Street and Bank Street with the Roods and Glengate. The photograph was taken when two-way traffic still flowed along the High Street, Bank Street and Glengate. A one-way system was introduced in the mid-1960s, but occasionally visitors who are not used to the traffic system cause chaos by accidentally driving down the street in the wrong direction.

Glengate gets its name because the roads from here lead to the Angus Glens. There have been many interesting buildings in the Glengate over the years, including a total of four churches on the three corners, which has led to this area being called Kirriemuir's 'holy corner'. These were the Seceder Hall, the North Free Church, the West United Presbyterian Church, and the Relief congregation's chapel. This chapel was built at the foot of the east side of the Glengate in 1792, and when its congregation moved to Bank Street United Presbyterian Church in 1832 Mr George Duke installed looms in the building. These were either rented out to weavers, or the weavers were paid wages while Mr Duke took the proceeds from the sale of their webs of cloth. William Duke converted the building into the Angus Mill in 1893, and it was used to produce oat flakes and animal foodstuffs until milling ceased in 1991. The building was finally demolished in 2002. William Low was born in Kirriemuir in 1858, and after taking over his brother's retail shop in Dundee in 1878 the firm of Wm. Low & Co. was born. The company gradually grew and at its peak owned many supermarkets throughout Scotland. It was absorbed by Tesco in 1994.

Reform Street and Post Office, Kirriemuir

203.469 (J.V)

The post office moved to Reform Street in 1906 when new premises, which it shared with the telephone exchange, were built there. Also found in Reform Street is the town hall and library. The hall was built in 1885 at a cost of £2,500 and an extension was made to house the library and a courthouse in 1913. During World War II the building housed Polish soldiers who donated the plaque that can be seen on the facade of the building.

The rest garden just beyond School Wynd on the Brechin Road was created in 1931 and dedicated to Sir J. M. Barrie. Another well-known landmark connected to Barrie on the same road is the house where he was born, which is open to the public. Just off Brechin Road stands a street named Tillyloss. The name probably derives from the much older *tulach-lios*, which is Gaelic for a rounded knoll with a habited enclosure. Thus it has been suggested that there has been a settlement on this piece of land for thousands of years, perhaps at least since the Iron Age in the form of roundhouses. The name Kirriemuir is Gaelic/Pictish in origin and can be translated as 'Mary's church quarter'.

GENERAL VIEW OF KIRRIEMUIR
FROM NEAR THE WINDOW IN THRUMS
2683.

This picture of Kirriemuir shows the eastern portion of the town from the Commonty, with the Hill cemetery in the distance. The Commonty lies between the Gairie Burn and the Forfar Road and became Kirriemuir's common land in 1835. For many years it was used as the bleaching and public clothes-drying green, but now often provides an exciting challenge for sledges during snowy weather.

Kirriemuir.

Winter.

Photographed from Bellies Brae on a snowy winter's day, the town looks very picturesque. There are regular heavy snowfalls in Kirriemuir during the winter months, often made worse by the town's proximity to the Glens, whose climate can be extremely harsh.

Kirriemuir from the North

The Hill of Kirriemuir provides a wonderful view of the town. The 'Stannin' Stane' on its summit suggests it was an important landmark thousands of years ago. Another site of interest which offers unique views over Kirriemuir and beyond is the Camera Obscura. This is one of only three in Scotland and is housed in the former cricket pavilion (see page 46) which was gifted to the town by Sir J. M. Barrie in 1930. A camera obscura is a darkened chamber with an aperture through which images of outside objects enter the room to be enlarged and projected onto a flat surface. The cemetery on the Hill was opened in 1858 and its most famous grave is that of James Barrie and his family.

This area of housing to the east of Kirrie Den (seen looking northwards) shows how houses and other buildings developed from medieval times with associated strips of land stretching behind them. The tower of St Mary's Church is in the background.

The David Smith Convalescent Home was given to the town in the 1920s by the son and daughter of David Smith. He was a stockbroker in Aberdeen who was born in Kirriemuir and left £16,000 in 1919 to fund a convalescent hospital in the town. The building was demolished in the early 1990s.

The Town House has had a long and distinguished history. It was built in 1604 and was the property of the Douglas and Angus Estates (the Douglas family were the Earls of Angus) until 1973, after which it came into the hands of the provost magistrates and councillors of Kirriemuir. Originally it had a forestair on its north side facing the square which led to the first floor. The ground floor was divided in two by a partition wall, and the west half was used as the town jail. The first floor

was the courthouse, which replaced the Court Hillock as the setting for Kirriemuir's regality courts. By 1833 the external stairway and upper floor entrance had been removed, to be replaced by an internal staircase and main doorway on the north side of the ground floor. At that time the jail and courtroom were both still in use, and the Town House was also used as the linen stamping office. Further architectural changes in 1862 included the addition of the curved bows to the north and west of the building, and a clock tower to the north. The clock was funded by public subscription. In 1896 the police station moved to premises in Reform Street and the post office was then situated in the Town House. Following its move to Reform Street in the early twentieth century the Town House was occupied by a number of businesses including Kidd's chemists and James Norrie, printer and stationer. It was transformed into Kirriemuir Gateway to the Glens Museum in 2001.

W. B. Mills' first bookshop, where Sir J. M. Barrie was reputedly introduced to literature, was on Bank Street. The shop then moved to the High Street and when the Albion Stores took the premises over in March 1933 Mills moved to the Town House. The Albion Stores were grocers and merchants selling hams and bacon, cheese, margarine, butter and jam, amongst other things. They continued to trade from their High Street shop until 1958. An advert in the *Kirriemuir Observer* in December 1923 listed their special offers and said 'Don't 'listen in', 'walk in' and share in the money saving lines we are offering'. Albion Stores competed with other grocers in Kirriemuir including James Duncan and James Kidd.

This hotel on the High Street was originally called the Crown Hotel. It became the Ogilvy Arms in 1898 when Archibald Campbell reopened it after refurbishment. At that time Campbell also owned the Airlie Arms Hotel, and attracted many visitors to his new premises not only by dint of the refurbishment but also because he had installed a gramophone. In 1923 the Ogilvy Arms, under new management, offered the traditional services of a hotel including 'Ample accommodation for commercial gentlemen and tourists', 'Motor and Horse Hiring', and 'Hearse and Mourning Coaches'.

St Andrew's Church on Glamis Road was built in 1903 on the site of the former South Free Church, dating from 1843. From 1929 it was known as the Livingstone Church. In the early 1960s it united with the South Parish Church to finally form St Andrew's. The South Parish Church had been built in 1835 to accommodate the growing population in the south of the Parish.

In 1974 Reform Street School celebrated its centenary. The school was built following the closure of the Parish School and other private schools, and at the time of its establishment in 1874 had around 400 children on the roll. When Reform Street School closed in 1977 its pupils began attending Northmuir Primary School. The buildings were demolished and Lyell Court sheltered housing complex was later built on the site.

This picture shows Northmuir in the early 1920s. Building in the area began in 1813 and many of the new houses were occupied by weavers and their handlooms. Areas of Northmuir were also given over to growing crops, especially potatoes and soft fruit including strawberries and raspberries. In the late nineteenth and early twentieth centuries Northmuir was a popular summer holiday destination. It increased greatly in size during the 1970s and new houses continue to be built in this area of Kirriemuir.

These cottages in Northmuir are fairly typical of the weavers' houses found there in the nineteenth century. Kirriemuir has been called the 'Little Red Town' because many of its buildings are made of a distinctive local red sandstone.

The Hill was given to the town in 1926 and for generations has a been popular place for children to play. There are many other parks in Kirriemuir including the Den, the Commonty and Davidson Park, which is to be found in Southmuir. It is named after James Davidson, who gifted the land to the burgh in 1923 to be used for all time as a public park. Martin Park is on Westmuir Road and has been the scene of many hard-fought football matches. It was given to the town in memory of George Martin of Kirriemuir.

From 1826 onwards many weavers' cottages were built on the Southmuir, which was also later called the Newtown. The Newtown (later shortened to Newton) Hotel had a chilling episode in its history when in 1890 its owner was charged with poisoning his wife between 28 July and 5 August that year. The trial was due to begin on 16 January in Edinburgh, but had to be postponed because a key witness, Mr James Peacock, failed to turn up. Mr Peacock had been a barman at the Newtown Hotel. A search was conducted back in Kirriemuir and Mr Peacock was found dead in a pond in the town. His death was said to be an accident due to his nervousness about speaking in court. After the trial in February Mr Webster was found not guilty of his wife's death and later left the country.

The village of Westmuir was developed in 1815 following the division of the muirland around the town which led to the development of Northmuir in 1813 and Southmuir in 1826. The school at Westmuir was built around 1863 and used until 1953. An area called Cloisterbank is situated near Westmuir and in 1783 local weavers and farmers had a disagreement there. That year the crops were of very poor quality and very scarce and the weavers thought that the farmers were keeping the scarce corn for themselves and inflating prices, so they raided their stores. This led to a fight at Cloisterbank where the weavers won a short-lived victory. The ringleaders were tried for their involvement although one lady, Elspet Mann, was made famous by her fighting performance for the weavers.

This picture shows a crowd gathered for the opening of Kirriemuir Golf Club's new clubhouse in 1910. The original golf club on the Hill was dissolved in 1908 and Kirriemuir Golf Club Ltd. formed as its successor. A 9-hole course was opened in 1909, and under the guidance of James Braid this was extended to 18 holes in the mid-1920s. During World War II potatoes were grown on holes 3 to 8.

Many sporting events took place on the Hill in Kirriemuir including celebrated cricket matches. The Allahkbarries XI was a team originally created by Sir J. M. Barrie comprising celebrities and famous cricketers. The team played against Kirriemuir Cricket Club in 1930 and again in 1973, and included journalist Ron Thompson and various Scottish internationals such as J. G. Laing. The match in 1973 raised funds for Barrie's Birthplace which is owned by the National Trust for Scotland. The team's name derived from the Arabic *Allah-akbar*, meaning 'may heaven help us', and Barrie's surname.

During the winter the ground of the Den used to be flooded and the frozen surface used for skating. In the late 1960s this practice stopped and outdoor skating in Kirriemuir ceased.

Kirrie Den is a haven for many leisure activities, and during the summer months putting in the Den has always been very popular.

Kirriemuir has a long history of musical associations; here the Kirriemuir Pipe Band are shown after winning a competition held at Crystal Palace in 1912. Many other well-known and skilful musicians have originated from the town. These include Jim Cameron and Ronald Scott. The latter was born in Kirriemuir in 1946 and became lead singer with the rock group AC/DC. Scott's family emigrated to Australia in 1952. Called Bon rather than Ronald, Scott joined AC/DC in 1974 and contributed greatly to their worldwide success before his premature death in 1980. He is remembered as an enigmatic and truly talented musician by fans around the world.

Every year the opera was a great affair. This picture shows the cast of *HMS Pinafore* in 1905.

Kirriemuir's original station opened in November 1854 but the building in this picture dated from 1871. The short branch to Kirrie closed to passengers on 4 August 1952 and to goods traffic on 21 June 1965, although this photograph, showing an enthusiasts' special (a service specially laid on for railway enthusiasts) was taken on 23 April 1962 looking west to the buffer stops of the station terminus. The Met–Cammel built type 26 diesel locomotive has been detached from its train so that it can loop round it and pull it away from the station in the opposite direction. The buildings and the track still appear in pristine condition despite not having seen a revenue-earning passenger train for a decade.

Kirriemuir, E. End

63632

The presence of a railway station in Kirriemuir was a great boost to commerce in the town, especially benefiting the textile industry. Many goods were transported to and from Kirriemuir en route to Stewart & Ogilvy's Gairie Linen Works, which opened in 1872 on Bellie's Brae, and Wilkie's Kirriemuir Linen Works, which opened in the late 1860s on Marywell Brae.

A THRUMS WEAVER

For generations the working lives of many families in Kirriemuir revolved around the handloom. A large number of weavers were involved in the Chartist movement, which aimed to reform Parliament and extend the right to vote. This political activism contributed to Kirriemuir's weavers' riot of 1839. Manufacturers announced that there was to be a reduction in the price paid for a weaving web, and therefore a reduction in weavers' wages. Following a heated meeting, some weavers attacked a group of manufacturers returning from Dundee on horseback. The sheriff and 70 constables attempted to calm the situation but had to take refuge in the Town House. Only the arrival of soldiers of the 72nd regiment from Dundee ended the riot.

J. & D. Wilkie's Kirriemuir Linen Works opened in the late 1860s. Steam-powered looms meant that textile production could take place on a large scale, but the development of big, private factories such as Wilkie's was predated by so-called 'manufactories' in the town where individual weavers shared workplaces. The idea of the manufactory had its origins in Edinburgh and Glasgow in the seventeenth century. Wilkie's factory was situated on Marywell Brae. The ancient Mary Well was located near the brae and along with the Lady Well provided Kirriemuir with much of its water.

SONS O' SCOTIA'S SOIL   BACHELOR LIFE NEAR KIRRIE.

The lives of agricultural workers have never been easy, but they often had a great sense of camaraderie. The fertile land around Kirriemuir ensured that farming had a great influence on the town. Sheep and hill farming have formed the basis of the economy of the Glens for thousands of years, supported by other activities dependent on the land including deer stalking and shooting, fishing, and forestry.

Birthplace of J. M. Barrie, Kirriemuir

James Barrie was born at 9 Brechin Road on 9 May 1860, and in later life achieved fame as an author and playwright. When his birthplace was placed on the market in 1937 it was purchased by a private individual who presented it to the National Trust for Scotland to ensure its long-term survival. After the tenant and caretaker died in 1963 restoration was carried out, and Barrie's Birthplace officially opened to the public.

Residence of J. M. Barrie, Kirriemuir 46096. JV.

James Barrie's father David had been a weaver, but in 1854 took a clerical job in a linen factory in Forfar and moved his family there. In 1872 he returned to Kirriemuir to work at the Gairie Linen Works, and the Barrie family moved into the top apartment of a house called Strathview on the corner of Glamis Road and Forfar Road. This was owned by James's uncle David Ogilvy. James returned regularly to Strathview, and it was here in 1894 that he married the actress Mary Ansell. Their marriage ended in divorce in 1909.

In the novel *A Window in Thrums* Barrie describes 'the house on the brae', which was a little white dwelling he could see from the window of Strathview. Barrie used 'Thrums' to describe Kirriemuir in his novel, and the name has become synonymous with the town. Thrums were actually threads that were the saved from the ends of webs of cloth. They hung on the ends of looms and were used to join old and new webs together.

Window in Thrums, Kirriemuir

The small white cottage standing across from James Barrie's family home, Strathview, has been a popular photographic subject since it was made famous in his novel *A Window in Thrums*, published in 1889. Kirriemuir's most famous son has been responsible for attracting many visitors to the town.

Following his success as a playwright and author, Sir J. M. Barrie based himself in London. However, he frequently returned to both Kirriemuir and the house of his birth, which he is seen standing outside in this picture (Barrie is in the centre). On more than one occasion he rented a house for the summer in the beautiful Glens of Prosen and Clova.

Just behind Barrie's birthplace is a wash house which he made famous as 'Wendy's house' in the story of Peter Pan. It was used by Barrie as his first theatre when he was a child.

Local people often felt uneasy about the presence of gypsies in the area – this picture of a gypsy family was taken at Caddam Wood in Kirriemuir. Today Caddam Wood is a very popular place for walking and enjoying picnics. In *Little Minister* Sir J. M. Barrie mentioned a road which runs through the wood called Windyghoul Road. The remains of a Roman Road also run through Caddam Wood and this road might have been used to connect the three late first century AD Roman forts of Cardean (near Meigle), Castlehill (Inchewan), and Stracathro (near Edzell).

Gipsy Life.

The Sports Pavilion on the Hill, Kirriemuir.
(The Gift of Sir J. M. Barrie to his Native Town).

2663.

Sir J. M. Barrie gifted the sports pavilion on the Hill to the town of Kirriemuir when he was made the first and only Freeman of Kirriemuir in 1930. It now houses a Camera Obscura, and like Barrie's Birthplace is administered by the National Trust for Scotland. James Barrie is buried nearby in the Hill cemetery.

The Jubilee Arms Hotel at Cortachy is a popular summer retreat for visitors to the area. It was built in 1887 and reflected the popularity of this part of Scotland with visitors, who came from near and far to spend summer holidays near Kirriemuir. It is now called the Dykehead Hotel. The small village of Cortachy is rich in history. Cortachy Parish Church is an impressive building that was constructed in 1828 to replace the earlier post-Reformation church. Cortachy Castle is the property of the Earl of Airlie and holds a position of great strategic importance on the south side of the River South Esk.

Inverquharity Castle is situated three miles north-east of Kirriemuir and is one of the many castles in the area surrounding the town. Others include Balfour Castle, Clova Castle and Ballinshoe (Benshie) Castle, which are ruined. Some, like Cortachy Castle, Airlie Castle and Forter Castle are still inhabited and like Inverquharity are private residences.